YUK IT UP
WITH URKEL!

YUK IT UP
WITH URKEL!

Hilarious Urkel jokes,
silly sayings, riotous riddles,
far-out facts, and more!

C.M. Appleton

Special thanks to: Jean Feiwel, Bernette Ford, Sonia Black, Debbie Newberger, Veronica Ambrose, Karen McTier, Kelly Lindsey, Michelle Sucillon, Laurie Pessell and Carole Franklin.

Produced by Creative Media Applications

Writer: Eric Weiner

Art Direction: Fred Gates Design

ISBN 0-590-45745-4

12 11 10 9 8 7 6 5 4 3 2 1   2 3 4 5 6 7 / 9

Printed in the U.S.A.   40

First Scholastic printing, February 1992

YUK IT UP
WITH URKEL!

Dear Readers:

Guess what your pal Urkel has cooked up just for you. Yes, joke fans, it's my finest achievement, my magnum opus, my masterpiece, my piece de  resistance. Not only that, it's not half bad! (And it's more than half baked.) What is it? It's my very first joke book, *Yuk It Up with Urkel!* And I promise you right now, this fun-filled book will not be over your head. Unless of course, you hold your hands up really high while you're reading it! Hee-hee-SNORT! SNORT! SNORT! Yuk it up!

Yours,
Urkel

MY BIO—IN BRIEF

▲▲▲▲▲▲▲▲▲▲

Born: April 1, 1976. I begin wearing suspenders and glasses: April 1, 1976.

My Accordion Debut: May 3, 1980. "Child Prodigy Plays Polka at Carnegie Hall!" That's what the headlines all said. I have to admit, I was great. I played "Pig in the Polka," "The James Polka," and "Watch Out He Don't Polka You in the Eye." Then I got one of my suspenders caught in the stage curtain. The other suspender got caught in my accordion. When I played the next chord, I, er, brought down the house!

I fall in love for the first time: September 21, 1986. It was my first day in a new school. Suddenly I saw a vision of loveliness: Laura Winslow. She was getting a drink at the

bubbler. I was carrying a huge stack of books. I put the books down on the floor in front of me and ran toward her. And that's how I, um, *fell* in love.

My first kiss: July 6, 1987. I was at the petting zoo. I made the mistake of sticking my head into the llama's cage.

Prizes: December 6, 1988. First Place in the Walter F. Squinchell All-Chicago Science Fair for my simulation of a volcano erupting.

Made Front Page News: December 15, 1988. For blowing up the north side of Chicago with a volcanic eruption.

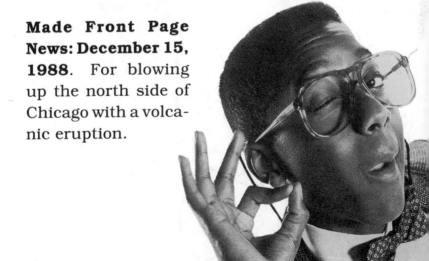

SPECIAL DELIVERY

I should have known I was in trouble. The moment I was born, the nurse held me up for my mom to see and Mom said, "Did I do that?"

Like all babies, I came into the world kicking and screaming. Of course, as soon as my mom got a look at me, she started doing the same thing.

The doctor told my mom it was an easy delivery. All he had to do was yank on my suspenders and I arrived.

My mother says there was a tragic mix-up at the hospital. To this day, she still worries that she may have ended up with the right baby!

Even as an infant, I was kind of short. I remember when I first started walking. Nobody knew.

LAB NOTES

Whenever I have time, I don my spanking white labcoat and pop down to my basement laboratory to cook up a new science experiment. Guess what? Last week little ol' *moi* discovered a way to super freeze ice cream so it won't melt! The only trouble is, you have to scoop it out with a flamethrower.

For a peek at some of my other amazing discoveries, feel free to browse through my lab journal.

Monday —

Wow! Three new speed records:

My pet mice, Albert and Einstein, raced through their maze and found the cheese in just 23.4 seconds. Then they raced upstairs and found my mother's guacamole dip in 48.6 seconds. And then my mom screamed and chased me out of the house in 11 seconds flat.

Wednesday —

My bread mold and fungus are developing beautifully. I left the petri dish in the kitchen to show my dad. He thought it was an appetizer and ate it.

Idea for a new experiment: Try to develop something for people who throw up after eating bread mold and fungus.

Friday —

Today I successfully recreated the famous experiment of dropping a pound of rocks and a pound of feathers from a great height. I dropped both out of our second floor window. Just as I predicted, the two bundles landed at exactly the same time. The next time I do this experiment, however, I must first make sure there is no one down below.

Sunday —

Gadzooks! I've done it. I've managed to cross ragweed with Kleenex, thus causing and curing hay fever at the same time!

Tuesday —

Gee, I thought I had discovered a new moon. Now I find out that the calibrations on my telescope were way off and I was pointing it into the Winslows' bedroom. Wait till Mr. Winslow finds out that the photos I published in our local paper are of the top of his head!

URKEL'S SONGBOOK

(All sung to the tune of Camptown Races, of course. Is there another tune?)

WHILE TAKING A MULTIPLE CHOICE TEST IN CLASS

True, true, false, false, false, false, true,

Doo-dah, Doo-dah,

The history of Waterloo,

All the doo-dah day.

Everybody finished fast,

Everybody passed,

But the principal's keepin' me after school,

For singin' the answers in class!

WHEN YOU'RE WAITING FOR THE BULLY WHOM YOU CHALLENGED TO A FIGHT IN THE PLAYGROUND AFTER SCHOOL

I take no guff from anyone,

Doo-dah, Doo-dah,

Not even a kid who weighs a ton,

All the doo-dah day.

I'll get beaten to a pulp,

Before I have time to gulp,

But I'll simply never run,

So somebody call 911!

WHEN I'M VISITING THE HOUSE OF MY BELOVED

Knockin' on the Winslows' door,

Doo-dah, Doo-dah,

Make a noise they can't ignore,

All the doo-dah day.

I'll play my accordion,

And howl just for fun,

I know my visit they'll never scorn,

Even at three in the morn!

TO BE SUNG LOUDLY IN THE FI-NAL SECONDS OF A CLOSE BAS-KETBALL GAME WHEN YOUR TEAM IS AT THE FOUL LINE AND ABOUT TO SHOOT...

Our team will win if he makes this shot,

Doo-dah, doo-dah,

Our team will lose if he does not,

All the doo-dah day.

Now he gives me a look,

He seems to be all shook,

And now he...totally blows the shot,

Uh oh, did I do that?

THE JOKE'S ON ME

▼▼▼▼▼▼▼▼▼▼▼▼

Q: Name the famous novel in which a person drinks a magic potion and turns into a killer.

A: *Dr. Jurkel and Mr. Hyde.*

Q: How long did the hippo sit on Steve?

A: Until he cried "Urkel!"

Q: What character did Steve play in his guest appearance on *Star Trek*?

A: Captain Kurkel.

Q: What's Steve's favorite underwater sport?

A: Snurkeling.

Q: What American coin was minted in honor of Steve?

A: The nurkel.

Q: Why did Steve's heartthrob, Laura Winslow, check into the hospital?

A: To get an urkelectomy.

Q: How does Steve's mom make coffee?

A: In a purkelator.

▼▼▼▼▼▼▼▼▼▼▼▼▼

Q: What does Steve's dad say when Steve tries to get out of doing his chores?

A: Quit shurkeling!

Q: How does Steve's family celebrate the Fourth of July?

A: With spurkelers.

Q: From what Greek hero is Steve descended?

A: Hurkeles.

ASK URKEL!

Dear Urkel,

I really like this girl in my class, but she won't give me the time of day. What should I do?

Dweeb City

Dear Dweeb City,

My advice to you is, purchase a watch! That way you will not need to depend on this inconsiderate classmate.

Urkel

Dear Urkel,

Everyone says I'm really beautiful and, you know, "hot"! I'm always getting asked out. But I can't decide who I should pick.

Too Many Choices

Dear Choices,

No sweat, my pet! I've got the solution to all your problems. Unfortunately, space does not allow me to give you the full answer now. So meet me by the jungle gym 15 minutes after school lets out, and I'll tell you personally.

Urkel

Dear Urkel,

I'm going out with this really cool sexy guy, Keith Morris. He's so rad! But last week, I caught Keith at the movies with my best friend, Stacy. I want to break up with him, but I still love him like crazy. What should I do?

Torn in Two

Dear Torn in Two,

Don't rip yourself apart. Urkel is here. What you need to do is make this Morris creep burn with jealousy. I know just the way to do it. Meet me by the jungle gym, about an hour after school, and we can discuss matters more fully.

Urkel

Dear Urkel,

What's your favorite kind of music?

Cindi

Dear Cindi,

Because I am a cool and hip dude, I, of course, groove on polka. But it's the music of love that is really music to my ears. How about a romantic slow dance as I play the soothing tunes of the accordion into your lyric-loving earlobes?

Urkel

HOW TO DRESS LIKE THE COOLEST—ME!

Some people say I dress too fancy. But that's only for really formal events, like school. Hee-hee-SNORT! This poster shows me in my play clothes, which are perfect for any really casual situation. Like when I'm alone in my room doing my homework!

I wear such big glasses that no one calls me "four-eyes." They call me eight-eyes.

A cardigan sweater is a must item for all truly cool dudes. Just look at Mr. Rogers. You can't get any hipper than that!

Even when I'm playing, I like to keep my polo shirt buttoned up all the way. Well, sometimes I unbutton the top button, but that's only in really really casual situations. Like when I go to bed.

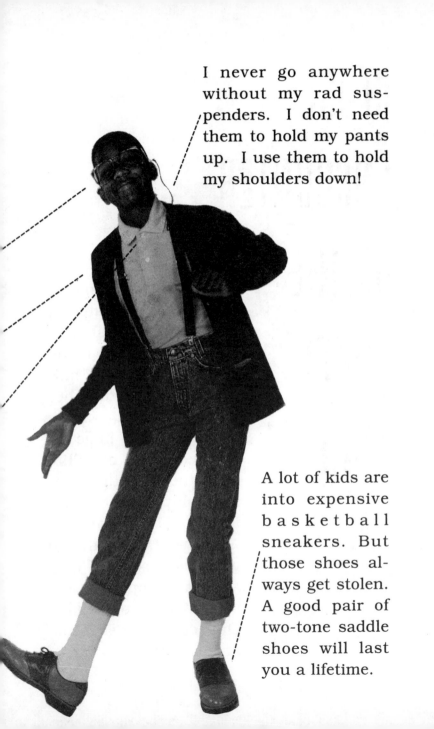

I never go anywhere without my rad suspenders. I don't need them to hold my pants up. I use them to hold my shoulders down!

A lot of kids are into expensive b a s k e t b a l l sneakers. But those shoes always get stolen. A good pair of two-tone saddle shoes will last you a lifetime.

CLOSE ENCOUNTER OF THE URKEL KIND

I was hurrying down Main Street, trying to catch up with Laura Winslow. (I kept shouting her name, but she must not have heard me.) Suddenly I heard a strange noise overhead. This huge object seemed to be falling out of the sky! A tiny green spaceship crashed right in front of Joe's Pharmacy! A crowd immediately gathered around. Then the hatch opened. The spectators let out a gasp. Out came these short green people wearing

suspenders and glasses! "Excuse me," yelled someone in the crowd. "But does everyone on your planet dress that way?" "Of course not," replied the alien in a high-pitched nasal voice. "Only the Urkels!"

URKELISMS

A bird in the hand is better than egg on your face.

He who laughs last probably didn't get the joke.

People who live in glass houses shouldn't throw stones, and neither should anybody else!

The grass is always greener when you don't get the fertil-izer mixed up with the kitty litter. (Did I do that?)

I forgot to bring my lunch to school today. Then I made an even worse miscalculation. I purchased the school's hot lunch special. Meat loaf. Actually, it looked like the meat had done more than loaf. It looked like it had quit permanently! I took one bite and started to choke. Luckily, my old friend Fuffner happened to see my plight. At least, I think he did. He grabbed me around the stomach and squeezed the breath right out of me. But that's what he does whenever he sees me. I was still choking. But then along came Waldo. Waldo started kissing my watch. That made me laugh. I laughed so hard I giggled that piece of meat right out of my throat. "Waldo," I said, "you're a Life Saver. Either cherry flavor or strawberry, I'm not sure which. But tell me, why were you kissing my watch?" Waldo looked at me, surprised and confused. "I was doing the 'time-lick maneuver.'"

THE SICK SENSE

I've never had hypochondria, but I'm always worrying that I might come down with it!

All my life I've had terrible insomnia. But only during the day.

I worry about death a lot, even though I'm just a kid. After all, every one of my ancestors came down with it.

My dad's a doctor...but he says I'm living proof that he can't cure everything.

The last time Laura had the flu, I swore to stay by her side until she got well again. That cured her immediately.

Waldo: Quick! Take me to the nurse's office!

Urkel: What is it?

Waldo: It's the room where the nurse works. How dumb can you get?

• The number of pistachio shells thrown out by Americans every day is double the number of nuts they eat!

• The people of Moli-Moli wear their underwear on the outside, but few people know it because they wear their clothes over them.

• In Fungoland, people are known as left-handed if they scratch their right ear with their left hand. If they scratch both ears at once, they're known as itchy.

• It takes two to tango but only one to play the accordion.

• The polka was a dance invented by a woman named Dot.

• People with glasses see much better when they actually put their glasses on.

1.

While your fellow classmate is desperately struggling to come up with the answer to a question, raise your hand way up in the air and shake all over with excitement. Yell, "Oo! Oo! Oo! I know! I know! That's so easy! Oh, please call on me! Oo! Oo! Pleasey-pleasey!"

URKEL'S GUIDE

2. Remind the teacher he or she forgot to give the homework assignment.

3. Finish really hard tests in three minutes and sit twiddling your thumbs and whistling "Camptown Races" while the rest of the class racks their brains trying to get the answers.

4. Come in late (but before the teacher arrives) and shout, "Okay, everybody, books under your desk. This is a quiz!"

0 CLASSROOM ETIQUETTE

URKEL'S MAGIC TRICKS

The Floating Chinese Vase. Suggest to your mother that her priceless Chinese vase would look better on the bookshelf, instead of on the mantel. When you pick up the vase, she'll scream, "CAREFUL! DON'T DROP IT!" You scream in shock. And following her instructions to a tee, throw the vase *up* into the air. (Magician's note: I've found this trick only works briefly.)

The Vanishing Guests Trick. Have a friend give a rad rap party. When the party is going full swing, trip over the cord from the CD player, knocking the CD player to the floor with a smash. Then tell everyone not to panic, because you also have tapes for the tape deck. Which would people prefer, "Greatest Polka Hits of the 1940s"? or "Hawaiian Love Chants for the Ukelele"?

THE WOOING OF LAURA

Urkel: Oh, my little bowl of hominy, every time I see you my stomach turns somersaults of excitement.

Laura: That's funny. When I see you, my stomach turns, too.

Urkel: Oh, dearest Laura, my heart burns for you.

Laura: Well, that almost makes us even.

Urkel: Well, I've got to go to class. Tell me, my little Miss America, do you promise you'll miss me?

Laura: I promise I'll miss you as often as I can!

Urkel: Say, my little petunia. How about going to a movie this Saturday night?

Laura: What a good idea, Steve! And for you, let me suggest bowling.

Urkel: Hey, my top-of-the-charts hit single, with what song would you like me to serenade you?

Laura: How about the song of silence.

Urkel: Say, my little pin-up, how about a date?

Laura: No, thanks. I prefer pomegranates.

Urkel: Well, then can I walk you home from school?

Laura: Only if you stay the appointed 20 yards behind.

Urkel: Then can I at least call you tonight?

Laura: Sure, as long as you do it from your house without picking up the phone!

Urkel: Hey, Laura, my little sugar cone, how about coming with me to the ice cream parlor?

Laura: I wouldn't go with you if you paid me $1,000,000.

Urkel: Then I guess $50 is out of the question.

EUREKA!

Welcome to the Steve Urkel workshop, birthplace to hundreds of handy-dandy inventions. Why, my mind is a regular popcorn popper of ideas! Here's but a small sample of the gadgets I've created...

- A machine that writes on the chalkboard 100 times at once: "I will not make goo-goo eyes at Laura Winslow during class." (I find I use this at least once a day.)

- A pair of electric shoes that automatically do the Urkel Shuffle. (It's important not to set these shoes on "high." If you do you'll start doing the Urkel Twitch.)

- An X-ray nut detector that tells you which candies have nuts in them before you bite in.

- Giant springs that you can attach to your sneakers when you need to vault over the leather horse in gym. (The one time I tried these, they worked a little too well. Luckily, I landed in the basketball hoop.)

- Windshield wipers for eyeglasses. They help me, because whenever I think of Laura Winslow, my glasses steam up!

- A system of electric wires that melts the snow off your sidewalk without you having to use the ol' shovel. (I was worried that the wires wouldn't generate enough heat. But the system performed so well it warmed my heart. In fact, it warmed the whole house — and set it on fire. Did I do that?)

URKEL'S GUIDE TO PHYSICAL FITNESS

Listen up, my little triceps. I've found that with just minutes of exercise each day, I can maintain my sleek figure. Now you can do the same. Every day be sure to do at least one of the following:

1. Touch your toes ten times. (Or, touch your ten toes once, whichever you prefer.)

2. Do 50 standing push-ups. Extend those arms!

3. Without touching them, wiggle your ears!

4. Jog a mile in a minute. (First wait a full minute. Then run any speed you like.)

5. Do 200 chin-ups as well as chin-downs (this exercise is also known as "nodding").

6. And finally, to complete your workout, don't forget to do the Urkel Shuffle!

URKEL'S HOMEWURKEL

Okay, my little pencil sharpeners! See if you can wrap your minds around these mind benders:

1.

If Urkel asks Laura to go to the movies 6 times, to go out for ice cream 3 times, and to play miniature golf 2 times, how many times total will Urkel and Laura go out?

Answer: 0.

2.

Laura and Urkel are riding on the school bus going 35 m.p.h. Urkel gives Laura a quick smooch on the cheek. Now, compute the speed of the bus.

Answer: 0 m.p.h. (Laura will scream. The bus driver will bring the bus to a complete stop.)

3. In the course of a 10-game season, the varsity football team plays each team in the league twice, and the Bluejackets win 5 games out of town and 4 games at home. Is it possible for another team to have a better record?

Answer: What does this have to do with Urkel?

4. Urkel's class takes a test. The second highest score is a 68. The lowest score is a 3. Urkel gets an 89. If the teacher grades on a curve, what will Urkel get?

Answer: Yelled at by his class-mates.

THE WORLD'S MOST FAMOUS

QUOTATIONS

To be or not to be...picked
last in gym.
– **William Urklespeare**

Do be a do be, don't be a
don't be, doo dah, doo dah!
– **Urkel on *Romper Room***

What goes up must come
down right smack on
somebody's head.
– **Urkelonymous**

All men are created equal,
except some have to wear
glasses.
–**Thomas Jefferson Urkel**

What light through yonder
window breaks? (Did I do
that?)
– **Romeo Urkel**

URKEL'S CHOICE

THE WORLD'S TOP TEN SNAPPY COMEBACKS

Has anyone ever insulted you? Believe it or not, it's happened to me. But I look at it this way: I'm glad when anyone takes the trouble to send their thoughts my way. And besides, an insult gives me a chance to fire back a zinger! Here are my top ten favorites:

10. Gee, you're a thimble of laughs.

9. Say, you're more fun than a barrelful of scorpions.

8. Wow—your wit is as sparkling as old soda pop.

7. My, you're sharp as a basketball.

6. You're just a joke a day.

5. You're quick as a molasses drip.

4. Don't quit your day job.

3. Easy, my funny bone is still sore from your last attempt at humor.

2. You know, with a mind as quick as yours you could get a speeding ticket—for holding up traffic.

1. Oo, funny *isn't* the word!

ODDS
AND
ENDS

I asked my father what life on the moon was like. He offered to buy me a one-way ticket.

People say that I'm accident prone. But I tell them that most of my accidents occur when I'm standing up!

Q: What's it called when you do the Urkel Shuffle in a china shop?

A: Break dancing.

I don't mind gym class, except on those days when I don't have an excuse from home.

PUNNY YOU SHOULD

▶ The other day I made a joke and there was such silence, you could hear a pun drop!

▶ I made another joke and everyone groaned. I guess some people think my puns are groan tiresome!

▶ *But I can never resist a good punneroo. And speaking of puns...*

What do you call the science of soda pop?
Fizzics.

What do you call the science of yawning and gasping?
Sighcology.

What happens if everyone does their algebra on the same piece of paper?
You make a big math.

What kind of clothes do cells wear when they're feelin' sad?
Blue genes.

PUNS ON PUNS

When was the first joke told?

Once a pun a time.

Who was the greatest jokester in all the fairy tales?

Rapunzel.

What did the jokester do every time he got the ball in the football game?

He punted.

Where do jokes come from?

Punsylvania.

Why did the joke writer write his riddles in pencil?

He ran out of puns.

▲▲▲▲▲▲▲▲▲▲▲▲▲▲▲